NII KWEI'S DAY

To the futures of Nii Kwei and his friends, and all the schoolchildren in Ghana.

First published in Great Britain in 2001 by Frances Lincoln Limited,
4 Torriano Mews, Torriano Avenue, London NW5 2RZ

British Cataloguing in Publication Data available on request

ISBN 0-7112-1769-6

Designed by Sophie Pelham

Printed in Singapore

1 3 5 7 9 8 6 4 2

AUTHOR ACKNOWLEDGEMENTS
Catherine McNamara and Francis Provencal would like to thank Nii Kwei Sanniez and his parents,
Mr William Nii Dodoo Sanniez and Miss Gladys Adams, his sisters and brother, Wilhemina Naa Adjeley,
Laureen Odua and William Nii Dodoo, Nii Kwei's grandfather, Mr Theodore Dowuona-Hyde
and other family members on the compound. We would also like to thank Mr Kwadwo Osei-Nyame
at the School of Oriental and African Studies at London University for checking the text.
A special thanks to Nii Kwei's schoolteacher and to his friends, to Abdul-Kadir Musa Mohammed
and to Nana Ampem Darko III, Chief of Nkonya.

NII KWEI'S DAY

From Dawn to Dusk in a Ghanaian City

Francis Provencal and Catherine McNamara

FRANCES LINCOLN

AUTHOR'S NOTE

Nii Kwei (pronounced 'Nee Kway') lives with his family in Accra, the capital of Ghana. They share a large old family home within a 'compound', an enclosed area where people can play, talk, do their chores and spend time together. Nii Kwei's compound is shared by several different families, but everyone knows everyone else and they all look after each other.

Some compounds have small businesses attached to them, like a tailor's shop or a a big outdoor oven for making cakes and pastries. Outside the compounds, nearly every street corner in Accra has its own 'chop bar' where you can buy delicious soups or stews. When people don't have time to cook, they go to the chop bar and sit down to eat at one of the benches, or they take food back to their compounds in a saucepan they've brought from home.

Although Nii Kwei's compound has a constant water supply, many children in the rural areas of Ghana do not have running water at home. For these children, gathering water takes up much of their playing and studying time.

AFRICA

Ghana

Henry Nii Kwei Sanniez – Nii Kwei for short – is seven years old.

He lives with his family in Ghana, a country in West Africa which is famous for its gold, cocoa, beautiful coastline and friendly people. Nii Kwei's family belongs to the *Ga* people, one of the main groups of people in Ghana.

GA people live along the coastal region around Accra. They are traditionally fishermen (not surprisingly, fish is still a favourite Ga food). Ga is also the name of the language they speak.

Nii Kwei's family live in a large old house not far from the sea. It is Nii Kwei's job to sweep the compound (the enclosed area outside the house) every morning. At half-past five, when it is still cool, he is already hard at work with his straw broom.

When his work is done,
Nii Kwei has a bucket bath.
Like most children in Ghana,
he washes outside.

Nii Kwei's bath doesn't take
long. Even though Ghana is a
hot country, the water can still
feel cold, especially at this
time of the morning!

While Nii Kwei changes into his school uniform, his father catches up on local events in the morning newspaper. Today there is a big picture of the *Black Stars* on the front page.

THE BLACK STARS are Ghana's national football team, and they play at the Accra Sports Stadium near Nii Kwei's house. Nii Kwei and his friends often dream about playing for the Black Stars when they get older.

Nii Kwei's mother is busy in the kitchen, preparing sandwiches and warm chocolate milk.

As soon as Nii Kwei's little brother has brought in the chairs, the children sit round the table and have breakfast. Nii Kwei's mother checks that everyone has remembered to put their homework in their bags, and that they all have enough money for the canteen at lunch time.

After breakfast, Nii Kwei and his brother wave goodbye to Grandfather Dowuona. Grandfather Dowuona fought in the Second World War, and has more stories to tell than anyone else in the compound.

Before Ghana became an independent country in 1957, it was part of the British Empire. In support of Britain, Ghanaian troops fought alongside the British in the Second World War.

Nii Kwei and his brother and sisters travel to school by taxi. Their journey takes them past the Accra Sports Stadium and along the coast, where they often see fishermen hauling in their catch. Nii Kwei's father catches a taxi in the opposite direction, to his office in the financial district of Accra.

The first lesson today is maths. Like most of Nii Kwei's lessons, it is held in English. When Nii Kwei plays with his friends, they always speak in *Ga* or *Twi*, although they may mix in some English words too.

TWI is the most widely spoken language in Ghana, although it is not usually written down. Ghanaian schoolchildren learn to read and write in English.

Maths is Nii Kwei's favourite subject so he works hard to stay at the top of the class. When he is older, he would like to learn how to use a computer. The school doesn't have computers yet, but there are lots of communication centres in Accra where you can send e-mails and surf the internet.

After morning lessons, Nii Kwei and his two best friends meet up at the school canteen. They buy some *waakye* and *kenkey*, and then find a cool spot under the trees to sit and enjoy their food.

WAAKYE is made out of rice and beans and comes with a spicy sauce called shito, *which is made from crushed prawns and tomato. It is often eaten with boiled egg and fried meat or fish.*

KENKEY is made out of fermented cornmeal, which is wrapped in corn leaves and then boiled.

After lunch, Nii Kwei plays an exciting game of *Drop-Peter-Drop*.

DROP-PETER-DROP As the players chant "Drop-Peter-Drop", one player runs around the outside of the group with a stone, trying to drop it behind another player's back without him realising. If someone senses that a stone is about to be dropped behind him, he has to run as fast as he can around the circle. If the player with the stone catches him before he gets back to his position, he becomes 'Peter' and the game begins all over again.

When lunch time is over, one of the older boys swings a big silver bell to call everyone in for afternoon lessons. The bell was a gift to the school from the local church. The church is also paying for a new block to be built so that more children will be able to attend the school in the future.

Afternoon lessons are normally more informal, and today a student teacher has come in to help. He and Nii Kwei read together and talk about the world outside Africa.

Through the open windows, the class can hear the school marching band practising outside. They are trying out some new tunes for assembly in the morning.

After school, Nii Kwei goes to the market with his mother, father and brother. Nii Kwei's mother buys him some tie-and-dye material from Abrams' store so that she can make him some new shirts.

Cloth and cloth designs are very important in African culture. On special occasions, like the birth of a child or the death of a loved one, people wear particular colours or patterns because they have a special meaning.

As they are leaving, Nii Kwei's mother sees some beautiful glass beads at a stall across the road.

Beads are an important part of women's traditional dress in Ghana, and many Ghanaian families own beads that have been in the family for generations. The oldest Ghanaian beads were made in Europe and brought to Africa hundreds of years ago by traders, who exhanged them for valuable Ghanaian goods.

Back at the compound, Kwame the barber is busy with a customer.
He offers a wide range of hairstyles, each with a different price tag.

Nii Kwei has an environmental science project to finish by the end of the week. Accra is a big city with a large population, so everyone is aware of the importance of a clean and tidy environment.

Now it is Nii Kwei's favourite part of the day! The compound is very large so it is just right for football. The high walls which enclose the compound are useful, too, because they make it impossible to kick the football onto the road outside.

To get his breath back after the game, Nii Kwei sits down and watches his brother play *oware* with their friend Adotey.

OWARE is played with seeds (or stones) and a hollowed-out wooden board. Each player takes it in turn to pick up seeds in a special order. The player who manages to collect all the seeds is the winner.

Earlier in the day, Nii Kwei's mother took a bus to the Makola market in town to stock up on vegetables. She likes bargaining with the *Market Mammies* behind the stalls to make sure she gets the best price.

MARKET MAMMIES is the name given to the women who sell in the markets throughout Ghana.

While Nii Kwei is playing in the compound, his mother chops up the *okro* that she bought in the market, and makes a big bowl of okro and goat meat soup for dinner.

OKRO *or okra is a small green vegetable which is often used in soups and stews. Okro soup is usually eaten with* banku, *a big ball of cooked cornmeal, and* cassava *(a starchy plant root). Like most meals in Ghana, people eat it with their hands, using the banku as a scoop.*

Over dinner, Nii Kwei tells his brother and sisters about his vegetable garden. He has planted some cassava and *yam* plants and two peppers. His sister promises to help him put up a fence around the garden in the morning, so that the chickens won't be able to scratch up the seeds.

YAM plants have starchy roots which can be cooked and eaten like potato.

22

After dinner it's time for bed. But Nii Kwei isn't tired yet so he reads some of his book. When he comes across something interesting, he calls down to his little brother in the bottom bunk, until they are both ready for sleep.

Wo odzogbaa, Nii Kwei. (Good night, Nii Kwei).

MORE ABOUT GHANA

The continent of Africa is made up of many different countries, each with its own traditions, languages and way of life. Ghana is in West Africa, and it has a long and beautiful southern coastline. The countries around it are the Ivory Coast in the west, Togo in the east and Burkina Faso in the north, which borders the vast, dry plains of the Sahara desert.

The cocoa business is very important in Ghana, and there are cocoa plantations all over the country. Cocoa plants have pods full of cocoa seeds, and these can be dried out and used to make chocolate. Ghana is also famous for its rich gold and diamond mines, which lie deep underground in the central area of the country. The Ashanti people who live in this region (called the Ashanti Region) wear beautiful jewellery made from the gold of the local mines.

It's hot in Ghana all year round, but people still notice the changes of season (especially if they take outdoor showers like Nii Kwei!). There is a very hot season from February to May, then a rainy season from June until August or September, and in December the *harmattan* arrives – during this time of year the Sahara desert to the north of Ghana sends down hazy, dusty skies and it starts to feel much cooler.

GHANA, THE PAST

When explorers from Europe first arrived on the sandy shores of Africa, they saw at once that they could use the land and its people to create great wealth for Europe. European businessmen started travelling to Africa to trade in goods like gold, ivory from elephants' tusks, and palm oil. They also traded in African people, who they sold to the rest of the world as slaves.

Eventually, after many wars and much pain for the African people, the continent of Africa was divided into 'colonies'. Ghana was colonised by Great Britain, (which is why the official language of Ghana is English).

In more recent times, African countries have gained independence from Europe. Ghana was the first African country ever to do this, becoming independent from Britain in 1957.

RELIGION IN GHANA

Ghanaian people have great respect for their ancestors, and they like to give thanks to them when something special happens, like the arrival of a new baby in the family or a good harvest. Christianity, which was introduced to Ghana by the Europeans, is also very popular, especially in the coastal regions. In the flat lands of northern Ghana, most people are Muslim.

PEOPLE IN GHANA

All the different peoples of Ghana have their own ways of doing things – the Ga people have different customs from the Ewe people, for example. They have their own favourite foods and their own language. But no matter what people they belong to, all Ghanaians place great importance on community and family life. Throughout Ghana, each community has a chief who makes decisions for the good of everyone in his care. If he is an Ashanti chief, he will speak to his people through a spokesperson, (called a 'linguist') and own a stool that is believed to contain all his powers. He will also wear a *kente cloth* (a brightly coloured, handwoven cloth) slung across his shoulders, because this is the traditional cloth of the Ashanti Region.

LANGUAGE IN GHANA

In Ghana, English is the language of the newspapers, the parliament and the national television stations. However, most people speak in one of the Ghanaian languages as they go about their daily lives.

TWI is the most widely spoken language in Ghana, and it is the main language of the Akan people. Akan people name their children after the days of the week. A boy born on Wednesday is called *Kweku*.

My name is Kweku. I live in Accra.

Me din de Kweku. Me te Nkran.

The FANTI people come from the west coast of Ghana. They are part of the Akan family, but they speak their own language, called Fanti. Fanti people also name their children after the days of the week. A girl born on Tuesday is called *Abena*.

My name is Abena. I live in Cape Coast.

Me diin de Abena. Me fii Oguaa.

GA people, like Nii Kwei and his family, live along the central coastal region of Ghana. In Ga language, a boy is called *Nii* and then a name chosen by his grandfather.

My name is Nii Torgbor. I live in Ako-Adjei.

Acho me Nii Torgbor. Min shia ye Ako-Adjei.

EWE people come from the Volta region of Ghana. Ewe speakers also name their children according to the day they are born.

My name is Afi. I live in Ho.

Nkonye nye Afi. Me tse Ho.

HAUSA is the language spoken by most people who live in northern Ghana. Hausa speakers are Muslim so they have Muslim names. Their first name is followed by the name of their father, and then the name of their grandfather.

My name is Abdul-Kadir Musah. I live in Salgar.

Sunana Abdul-Kadir Musah. Daga Salga nafito.

GLOSSARY

Akan – the Akan are the largest group of people in Ghana. Within the Akan, there are different groups, like the Ashanti and the Fanti

Ashanti – the Ashanti people live in Ghana's Ashanti Region. They are famous for their beautiful gold jewellery and ornaments, and their woven kente cloth

banku – cornmeal which has been cooked and shaped into a big ball

Black Stars – Ghana's national football team

cassava – the starchy root of the cassava plant. Cassava is often pounded together with green *plantain* (a kind of unripe banana) to make *fufu*, a popular Ghanaian dish

chop bar – a street bar where local food is sold

compound – in Ghana, and many countries in Africa, people's houses are walled off from the street. The area enclosed by these walls is called a compound

Drop-Peter-Drop – an exciting playground game

Ga – the Ga people are one of the biggest groups in Ghana. Ga is also the name of the language they speak

Harmattan – the name of a season in Ghana (and other countries around it), when dust is transported south from the Sahara desert, making the sky hazy and reddish all day, and the air very dry

kenkey – a popular dish made from cornmeal

kente cloth – a brightly coloured, handwoven cloth made by the Ashanti people

Market Mammies – the name given to the women who work in the markets all over Ghana

okro – a small green vegetable

oware – a popular game played with either seeds or stones and a hollowed-out wooden board

shito – a spicy sauce made from pounded dried prawns, spices and tomato, onion and garlic

Twi – the language spoken by most of the Akan people in Ghana

waakye – a popular breakfast or lunch dish that is often sold at chop bars

Wo odzogbaa, Nii Kwei – Good night, Nii Kwei

yam – the starchy root of the yam plant, which can be cooked and eaten like potato

INDEX